Test your, Dog's IQ

Published by Sourcebooks, Inc.
P.O. Box 4410, Naperville, Illinois 60567-4410
(630) 961-3900
Fax: (630) 961-2168
www.sourcebooks.com

ISBN-13: 978-1-4022-0895-9
ISBN-10: 1-4022-0895-2

Library of Congress Cataloging-in-Publication Data

Printed and bound in the United States of America.
SP 10 9 8 7 6 5 4 3

Do you find yourself bragging to friends and family about your dog's intelligence? Is your dog the kind of canine personality that is in a class by itself? Here is your chance to prove once and for all just how smart your dog really is. These fun exercises will seem like playtime to your dog, but will actually measure various facets of canine intelligence, alertness, adaptiveness, personality, memory, and sensory perception. As an added bonus, you have a chance to spend lots of time with your beloved pet.

The scoring system is simple:

- For every A answer, give your pup 5 points.
- 4 points for every B answer.
- 2 points for every C answer.
- 1 point for every D answer.

Consult the back of the book to score your dog once you have completed all the exercises. Who knows? You just might have a canine Einstein on your hands!

1 This exercise tests your dog's alertness. Grab one of his favorite toys and show it to him. While he is still watching you, toss the toy across the room behind his back. Does he...

A Retrieve the toy immediately

B Look around the room eagerly—then retrieve the toy within twenty seconds

C Stare at your hand expectantly, as if the toy were still in it

D Look around the room, find the toy, and eat it

2 Test your dog's physical intelligence with this fun exercise. You will want to take your dog to a park or open field where there is plenty of room to play. Bring either a ball or Frisbee with you. Toss the toy as far as you can and yell "Fetch!" to your dog. Does he...

A Run after the ball/Frisbee immediately (Add 2 bonus points if he catches it in his mouth!)

B Chase the toy after less than five seconds

C Ignore the game completely and go lie in the shade

D Chase the toy, but keep running past it

3 Show your dog a tennis ball and command her to sit in front of you. Pretend to throw the ball, but really let it fall behind your back. Does she...

A Retrieve the ball from behind your back

B Start in the direction you pretended to throw the ball, but return when she realizes her error

C Stay seated, waiting for you to throw the ball

D Run in the direction you pretended to throw the ball and bring back a bone she had hidden under the couch

4 Have someone outside let out a loud yell near the window where your dog is lying. When he hears the sound, does he...

A Begin to bark

B Growl from where he is lying

C Whimper and jump into your lap

D Continue sleeping

5 These next tests determine how well your dog communicates with you. Play fetch with him for ten minutes and then stop suddenly. Watch and see how he lets you know that he still wants to play. Does he...

A Drop the ball in front of you and pick it up repeatedly, his tail wagging

B Walk around with the ball in his mouth and his tail wagging

C Whimper and nudge your hand

D Go sit in the shade—ten minutes was enough anyway

6 Deliberately forget to refill her drinking bowl when it runs low. Wait and see how your dog tells you that she needs water. Does she...

A Go and find you and then beckon you over to the empty bowl

B Sit by her bowl and whimper until you take notice

C Find you and begin to whine

D Look for water in other places around the house and yard—rain puddles and toilet water are just as refreshing!

7 If there were a large bug flying around your house, what would your dog do?

A Watch it fly around, and only try to swat it with his paw when it is within striking distance

B Follow it around the house and try to swat it with his paw

C Run in the other direction—bugs are scary!

D Chase it around the house and try to eat it

8 Test your dog's social behavior. Baby-sit a friend or family member's cat when the person goes on vacation, or even just for a day. Notice how well your dog gets along with the cat. Does he...

A Approach it calmly, with interest

B Approach it with excitement

C Run in the other direction—cats are scary, too!

D Chase it around the house and try to eat it

9 Some night while watching television, notice how your dog reacts to an advertisement that features another dog barking. Does he…

A Stand up excitedly and bark in unison with the dog

B Watch with his ears up, but show no other signs of interest

C Stare blankly at the screen without getting up

D Run to the door and start growling

10 Test your dog's problem-solving skills. Put some dog food in her bowl at the time you usually serve her dinner. After she starts eating, interrupt by putting a magazine over the bowl. Take her out of the room for five minutes, then allow her to return to the bowl. What does she do?

A Immediately pushes the magazine out of the way and starts eating

B Sniffs around the bowl and whines a bit before pushing the magazine out of the way

C Doesn't find the food, barks at the bowl, then eats the magazine

D Become fascinated by the feature article on Lassie, but does not find the food

11 How many fundamental dog commands (e.g., "sit," "stand," "roll over," "lie down," "give me your paw," or "stay") does your dog know?

A More than five

B Three or four

C One or two

D None—but he could learn if he would just apply himself

12 Determine how verbal your dog is by keeping a log of his "vocabulary." Include a number of different barks, grunts, growls, whines, and other noises your dog makes on a daily basis. How many distinctive noises does your dog make to communicate with you?

A Twelve or more

B Six to eleven

C Two to five

D My dog prefers sign language

13
Crumple up a piece of scrap paper into a ball and throw it to your dog. Does he...

A Pat it with his paw to see if it's a real ball before bringing it to you

B Retrieve it and bring it back to you

C Ignore it

D Eat it

14
It is a proven fact that dogs have an accurate internal clock; they know when it's dinnertime, when their owners are due home from work, and when it is time to go to sleep. How accurate is your dog's internal clock?

A To the second

B About five to ten minutes off

C Fairly accurate

D What internal clock?

15
Play tug-of-war with your dog with a toy or piece of rope. After awhile, let go suddenly. How long does it take for your dog to let go of his end of the rope and realize the game is over?

A Less than five seconds

B Half a minute

C A minute or more

D He falls asleep that night with the rope still in his mouth

16 This exercise will test your dog's spatial orientation skills. Hide your dog's favorite treat in your pocket. Then, place a large mirror in front of your dog. While he is staring at his reflection, stand behind him and hold up the treat. Does your dog…

A Turn around immediately to grab his prize

B Sniff the mirror, and then turn around to claim his treat

C Sniff the mirror, and give up when he can't "find" the treat

D Start licking the mirror

17 If your dog usually sleeps on the bed with you throughout the night, what does she do when she first awakens?

A Becomes your personal alarm clock, licking your face and gently nudging your arm until you're awake

B Only nudges your arms and face after you're awake

C Jumps off the bed and whimpers softly at the bedroom door until you're awake

D Rolls over and falls off the side of the bed

18 During a severe thunderstorm, how does your dog react?

A Sits quietly close to you or on your lap

B Jumps restlessly from chair to chair until the thunder subsides

C Hides under the bed, shaking and whimpering even after the thunder has stopped

D Sits by the door that leads outside with a ball in his mouth. Thunder? What thunder?

19 While you are eating dinner, call your dog to your side. One at a time, throw down two separate scraps of meat to him. Then, the third time, crumple up a napkin and toss it to your dog. Does he…

A Keep looking at you, waiting for his real scrap of food

B Look at the napkin, lick it curiously, and then look up at you for more food

C Sniff the napkin and slink away, forlorn

D Eat the napkin, and then reach his paw onto the table to steal more treats

20 Rate how quickly your dog learns new tricks or commands:

A Very quickly—usually no more than a few days

B Within a week or two

C Within a month or two

D Intelligence isn't everything!

21 When you have your dog's full attention, reach behind you and tap a smooth, flat surface (e.g., tabletop, counter surface, etc.). Be sure that your dog can't see that you are making the noise. What does your dog do?

A Immediately perks his ears up to find the source of the sound

B Hears the sound, but goes into another room to find it

C Leaves the room looking bored

D Starts ramming his head against the wall to duplicate the sound

22 When the room is quiet and your dog is attentive, perk up suddenly and ask, "What's that?" Does your dog…

A Immediately perk up his ears to listen

B Look at you blankly

C Sigh and go to sleep

D Look at you with confusion, then grab his leash in his teeth

23 If you could describe your dog with one phrase, what would it be?

A Total genius

B Alert and active

C A bit on the slow side, but loveable

D A few cans short of a six-pack

24 You are walking in the park with your dog, and a large dog approaches you. How does your dog react?

A Barks once and watches the other dog alertly

B Sniffs curiously at the dog's feet

C Hides behind you and barks at the dog

D Starts humping the dog ecstatically

25 If your dog had a favorite magazine, what would it be?

A *Scientific American*

B *Field & Stream*

C *Good Housekeeping*

D *Sports Illustrated Swimsuit Edition*

26 If your dog had a favorite TV show, what would it be?

A *Lost*

B *Friends*

C *Touched by an Angel*

D *Fear Factor*

27 Which famous cartoon dog is most like your dog?

A Snoopy

B Underdog

C Goofy

D Scooby Doo

28 If your dog had a job, what would it be?

A Lawyer

B Administrative assistant

C Wal-Mart greeter

D Short-order cook—he can put the leftovers in a doggie bag!

29 In a classroom, which character would your dog be?

A Honor student

B Jock

C Teacher's pet

D Class clown

30 How does your dog typically behave when you take him for a walk?

A He keeps pace with you, stopping occasionally to sniff new and exciting things

B He lags a bit, but shows interest in his surroundings

C You have to pull at his leash constantly to keep him moving

D It's a game of tug-of-war between the two of you—he's always trying to break free

31 You sit down on the couch to watch a movie. What does your dog do?

A Sits quietly at your feet, watching the television

B Snuggles up against you immediately

C Wanders into the room halfway through the movie to join you

D Takes the opportunity to gnaw on the antique chair in your bedroom

32 When you take your dog with you in the car, what does she do?

A Sits in the front seat with you, poking her head out the open window

B Sits in the front and tries to put her head in your lap

C Snuggles up in the backseat with a favorite blanket

D You can't take your dog in the car—she tried one too many times to eat the steering wheel

33 You return home after a week of vacation. How does your dog react to you?

A Sniffs you curiously and wags his tail in greeting

B Wags his whole body ecstatically, jumps up and covers your face with kisses

C Keeps a safe distance until he sizes you up

D Thinks you're an intruder and growls at you

34 Once it is completely dark outside, turn out all the lights so that your house is as dark as possible. Call your dog's name. What does he do?

A Comes to you immediately

B Comes to you within thirty seconds

C Whimpers until you come to him

D Begins barking anxiously and crashing into walls, furniture, etc.

35 While your dog is watching you, walk out of the room and put on a scary mask. Wait ten seconds, and then return to the room silently. How does your dog react?

A Barks defensively, but realizes who you are after a few seconds

B Barks until you take off your mask

C Looks uninterested and takes a nap

D Wags his tail and pees on the carpet

36

In this exercise, you will test your dog's life-saving instincts. While your dog is watching, find a clear area of the floor and flop down (as if you were fainting). Remain completely still. How does your dog react?

A Barks loudly and rushes over to you, nudging you with his nose (5 bonus points if he knocks the phone off the hook and dials 911!)

B Whimpers and approaches you worriedly

C Watches you for a moment before walking away

D Rushes over to you and begins chewing on your leather shoes

37

At bedtime, close the door to your bedroom when you know that your dog is watching you. After five seconds, call his name. Does he…

A Approach the door immediately and begin to bark or scratch

B Plop down outside the door

C Make himself at home in the kitchen

D Get a running start and ram into the door several times before giving up

38

Give your dog a large bone. What does he do with it?

A Gnaws at it

B Buries it in the backyard

C Sniffs it for a minute and then walks away

D Scampers off in terror—what was that thing?!

.

39 Set up a baby gate or other barrier at the bottom of a staircase. Stand on the stairs with his favorite treat in your hand. Let him sniff it, then proceed to the top of the stairs and hold out the treat. What does he do?

A Barks excitedly and leaps gracefully over the barrier

B Sniffs the barrier and paws at it in hopes of knocking it down (1 bonus point if he succeeds!)

C Whimpers in frustration and walks away

D Gets his head stuck between the banister rails

40 Here's a canine "trick question" for your dog. Stand in front of your dog and, with the tone and body language you would normally use to command him to sit, substitute another word in the same authoritative tone (e.g., "tuna!"). What does your dog do?

A Sits immediately

B Looks confused, but sits after less than fifteen seconds

C Sighs and walks away in bewilderment

D Wags his tail and fetches his squeaky toy

41 While your dog is in another room, squeak his favorite squeaky toy. Before he sees you, quickly hide the toy. When your dog comes in, does he...

A Sniff around excitedly and find the toy within twenty seconds

B Sniff around excitedly and find the toy in under a minute

C Hover in the doorway with a look of confusion

D Come in carrying his leash in his teeth

42 If your dog were on a baseball team, who would he be?

A The coach
B The shortstop
C The bat boy
D The mascot

43 If you're in a field or meadow, what does your dog do when you unclip his leash?

A Bounds off to explore, checking in every few minutes so that you know he hasn't gone too far
B Stays close to you, but explores his surroundings
C Lies down and naps in the sun
D You wouldn't dare try—you'd never see him again

44 What would your dog's hobby be if he were a person?

A Crossword puzzles
B Playing tennis
C Sunbathing
D Watching reality television

45 When you take your dog to the vet, how does he behave with other animals in the reception room?

A Quiet, friendly, and attentive

B Barks a bit, but remains reasonably calm

C Clings to you apprehensively

D You can't sit in the waiting room with your dog since he tried to eat Mrs. Smith's hamster

46 You take your dog for some grooming. How does he behave once he's in the groomer's hands?

A Friendly and happy, as pliable as the groomer could hope

B A bit excited and apprehensive, but fairly amenable

C Frightened and skittish—most of the shampoo ends up on the floor instead of on his coat

D The groomer has to clamp his mouth shut so that he stops trying to drink the shampoo

47 How obedient is your dog when it comes to chewing things around the house?

A Perfectly obedient—she chews only on her toys

B Very obedient—once in awhile, she goes for a shoe or piece of paper, but stops when you scold her

C She needs more training—you still find shreds of paper or leather after she's been home alone

D Nothing's safe from this dog— she'd try to chew her own leg off

48 What would your dog's favorite class in school be?

A Calculus

B Gym

C Study hall

D Detention

49 If your dog were one of the following historical figures, who would he be?

A Benjamin Franklin—clever and revolutionary

B Thomas Edison—innovative and persistent

C Marilyn Monroe—beautiful and entertaining

D Larry, Mo, or Curly—classic slapstick comedian

50 Balance a throw pillow on your dog's head. How does she react?

A Walks across the room, balancing the pillow perfectly on her head

B Tries to balance it and looks apologetic when it falls off

C Acts startled, shakes it off, and looks at you like you're crazy

D Lies down and goes to sleep with the pillow over her head (deduct one extra point if she falls asleep standing up)

51 While your dog is attentive, leave your house. After a minute, knock five times at the front door. How does your dog react?

A Bounds to the door and sits expectantly, tail wagging

B Barks, comes to the door and paws at it intently

C Stays curled up on his bed; thumps his tail when you reenter

D After five minutes with no response, you reenter to find him busily digging through the garbage

52 While walking your dog, deviate from your normal route (e.g., take a right where you normally take a left). How does he react?

A Looks up at you curiously and barks a warning that you've gone the "wrong" way

B Tries to pull you in the right direction

C Doesn't seem to notice the change in routine

D Pulls you across the street to a new fire hydrant and marks his territory proudly

53 Who would your dog have been friends with in high school?

A The honor roll crowd

B The in crowd

C The jocks

D The rebels

54 Put on a CD or video of dogs barking (the *Jingle Cats* and *Dogs* CDs are perfect for this exercise). How does he react?

A Barks in perfect time with the recorded dogs

B Barks excitedly in response to the noise

C Whimpers and hides behind you

D Starts growling and attacks the CD player

55 How do your neighbors, friends, and family feel about your dog?

A They're in awe of his intelligence

B They can't wait to see your friendly, furry friend

C They hardly know him—he usually hides from them

D There's sure to be a funny story to tell when he's around

Scoring Key

Pure Genius

200–275

Consider your dog to be one in a million! Your canine friend has it all: physical intelligence, acute sensory perception, high adaptiveness, and a winning personality to boot. The sky is the limit when training a dog of such high intelligence—he is so in tune with his surroundings that you can teach him to do just about anything.

Loyal Companion

111–199

Your dog is an intelligent, loyal animal who will do his best never to let anyone hurt you. This dog is relatively easy to train, though some tricks may require time and patience to teach. The Loyal Companion will wait by the door for you to return home every day, and do not be surprised if you find him gazing at you adoringly. Take pride in this smart, affectionate dog!

Laid-Back Lassie

81–110

This dog may not be the most intelligent or adventurous, but she is also the least likely to yank at the leash during walks. The Laid-Back Lassie depends upon you for

protection and guidance, so be sure to give her lots of extra hugs. While she may not be the easiest to train, she is aware of her surroundings—sometimes so much so that she becomes nervous and turns to you for reassurance. Guard this precious gem with your life, and she will be sure to shower you with kisses!

Wild Thing

55–80

This dog can be quite the handful! Be patient and loving, and speak to him in soft, reassuring tones to calm him down when he becomes hyperactive. Although you may need to hide your best china from this dog, he really is fun to live with and is always full of surprises. You probably will not be able to teach the Wild Thing many tricks, but he will always provide you with lots of funny stories to tell at the next party!